D0743771

KLAONICA

KLAONICA is the Croat-Serbian for *slaughterhouse, abattoir, butchery, shambles.*

This anthology of poems is for the wounded and the weary and the dispossessed of Bosnia-Herzegovina, whether they describe themselves as Yugoslav, ex-Yugoslav, South Slav, Serb, Croat, Muslim, Jew, Catholic or Orthodox, Bosnian or ex-Bosnian.

Poetry may be only words. And politics too may be only words, words less truthful, less direct, less meaningful. War is another agenda.

This book is not made in anyone's interest or bias, but in whatever measure of solidarity is possible with the victims of this most vicious of wars. It is made in the hope of turning words into money, and money into bread for the starving, medicine for the sick, bandages, anaesthetics, whatever is needed to provide some comfort and some succour. A drop in the ocean of misery in the former Yugoslavia, it is what we can do as poets and as people.

May God bless us, and all who sing with us.

KEN SMITH
JUDI BENSON
Editors

SARAJEVO STREET MARKET

KLAONICA
POEMS FOR BOSNIA

EDITED BY
KEN SMITH & JUDI BENSON

BLOODAXE BOOKS

ISBN: 1 85224 283 3

First published 1993 by
Bloodaxe Books Ltd,
P.O. Box 1SN,
Newcastle upon Tyne NE99 1SN.

Bloodaxe Books Ltd acknowledges
the financial assistance of Northern Arts.

Cover printing by J. Thomson Colour Printers Ltd, Glasgow.

Printed in Great Britain by
Bell & Bain Limited, Glasgow, Scotland.

This nation has suffered too much from disorder, violence and injustice and is too used to bearing them with a muffled grumble, or else rebelling against them, according to the times and circumstances. Our people's lives pass, bitter and empty, among malicious, vengeful thoughts and periodic revolts. To anything else, they are insensitive and inaccessible. One sometimes wonders whether the spirit of the majority of the Balkan peoples has not been forever poisoned and that, perhaps, they will never again be able to do anything other than suffer violence, or inflict it.

IVO ANDRIĆ, 1892-1975,
Bosnia, Yugoslavia

from *Signs Bridges Conversations with Goya*
translated by Celia Hawkesworth & Andrew Harvey

CONTENTS

Realm of Darkness
A Serbian Folk Story

There is a story about an emperor who having reached the end of the world with his soldiers, set out for the Realm of Darkness where nothing can ever be seen; not knowing how he would be able to find his way back, the emperor left some foals outside so the mares would lead them out of the darkness back to the foals. And so they entered the Realm of Darkness, and walked on and on. Under their feet they felt small stones, and out of the darkness there came a voice: 'Whoever shall take some of these pebbles with him will regret it, and whoever takes none will also regret it.' Some of the men thought: 'If I shall regret it, why should I carry these stones?' and others again thought: 'I will take one at least.' When they returned to the world of light they saw the pebbles were precious stones; and so those who had not taken any were sorry they had not, and those who had, that they had not taken more.

VUK STEFANOVIĆ KARADZIĆ, 1787-1864
Serbia, part then of the Ottoman Empire

Posthumous Rehabilitation

The dead have remembered
our indifference
The dead have remembered
our silence
The dead have remembered
our words

The dead see our snouts
laughing from ear to ear
The dead see
our bodies rubbing against each other
The dead hear
clucking tongues

The dead read our books
listen to our speeches
delivered so long ago

The dead scrutinise our lectures
join in previously terminated
discussions
The dead see our hands
poised for applause

The dead see stadiums
ensembles and choirs declaiming rhythmically

all the living are guilty

little children
who offered bouquets of flowers
are guilty
lovers are guilty
guilty are poets

guilty are those who ran away
and those that stayed
those who were saying yes
those who said no
and those who said nothing

the dead are taking stock of the living
the dead will not rehabilitate us

1957

TADEUSZ RÓŻEWICZ
Poland
Translated from the Polish by Adam Czerniawski

Sarajevo Speaks:
I am an Island, in the Heart of the World

The world is vast, the continents float
and calamity lurches everywhere, but this is
different: the forest scent up north is the same
as the forest scent down south, and that scent is
unlike anything a man has yet heard of, seen, or touched.
In vain do the nostrils widen (is it the mother's womb
that maybe emits the same smell to an embryo?) – it is the smell
of Nothing that sings and cries with the same voice –
for love and calamity have the same countenance
here, and everything's identical. At the gates, guards
who feel a thrill, guards who dream
standing (of a Flight, a soft wanting
wing!) – but the same voice will rouse them all,
'Sarajevo! May the lightning strike you!' – It's someone
crying for my help again. A desperado and a wiseman,
a child, a vagrant, and a rogue – reconciled
before me: everything is equal here, everything
the same. I am an island, in the heart of the world,
nothing reaches me, only this languid
blood, only a thrill floating over everything.
Silence, and nothing all around.

ABDULAH SIDRAN
Sarajevo
Translated by Mario Suško

Clearing Up

All night long the angels with pipes fell out of the sky
the awls dipped into poison pierced our ear-drums
we hated everything alive, suicides smiled
from pill-bottles

But the day, so cruelly beautiful, came after that
(crowds everywhere, sterilised cotton, thermometers of icicles)
A dripping echo of honey-cakes burst into warty reality
from our childhood

And the hearts broad-jumped without saying 'jump'
and the picture frames of our dead ones put forth leaves
and every thing glittered with all its might
as if the world passed again through the filter of flood!

It seemed there was no place on earth for any villain
and that Pericles and Caligula were of the same clay
and the souls of our fellow-men were noble and pure
as in the obituaries!

That good threatened evil with an inescapable checkmate
and that everyone would be issued a visa to paradise
and that we, kinder than Francis of Assisi himself, wished
even to call a horse-whip brother!

MARKO VEŠOVIĆ
Sarajevo
Translated by Mario Suško

Small Town without Direct Railway Connection

To tell the truth, I have strong prejudices toward all blind,
cross-eyed, deaf people, toward those without legs, arms,
those hunchback ones, etc. I've noticed that there is a strange
relationship between man's appearance and his soul because
together with a lost member the soul seems to be losing a certain feeling.

— M.Y. LERMONTOV

1.

have you watched people dying what have you felt yes i have
watched i've felt fine watching people die can't complain

2.

have you been at the cemetery among different graves where men
are put in deep holes and others deliver speeches what have
you felt yes i have been there walked among the graves every-
where i've felt fine have no objections

3.

have you been to hospitals seen the sick that use drugs what
have you felt of course i've been there to all kinds of
hospitals and i have been amazed to see how nice it is there
comfortable quarters good food

4.

have you ever been to barracks among soldiers that want to
run away home have you seen them did you have a nice time yes
of course i have been to hospitals and front-lines there's
no place i haven't been to and i've felt fine couldn't be
better i've felt wonderful really was amazed why should i
hide my pleasant feelings

5.

have you been to concentration camps where they lock people
up and do not let them go anywhere and feed them poorly so
they grow thin and die tell me the truth how you felt all
right i'll tell you frankly i've been to concentration camps
everywhere nice barbed wire only hardly any fun so one might
get bored quickly other than that it has been fantastic people
from all over the world so you hear and learn about all sorts
of things

14

6.

have you been at the coast in summer drunk refreshing soft
drinks in the sun by the sea of love gone by boat with merry
and healthy people how have you felt there yes i've been there
and boy i barely managed to stand it did not like it a bit
couldn't wait to get back and never go there again i expected
a lot but it was utterly boring and people those rotten people
constantly want to do a bad turn to one another

AHMED MUHAMED IMAMOVIĆ
USA / Bosnia
Translated by Mario Suško

CHRIS RIDDELL / THE INDEPENDENT

The Warlords

The blackbird once believed
He cranked the sun up with his song

Likewise but with love
Quite inconspicuous women

Now the warlords crank and crank
Only graves come up

CHRISTOPHER MIDDLETON
Austin, Texas

Casualties

What is suffering?
We will tell you.

What is to be punished
for something you have not

done? We know it.
What is it to remember

bread as though it were
gold, water like an impulse

of silver? Who cares that
it is not our fault?

We were born to learn
we are invisible, inaudible

to those with a rich man's
cataract, a discreet ear.

R.S. THOMAS
Gwynedd

Concentration Camp

In special moments you suddenly feel one should not have talked
    of socrates
One should have talked of pigs. Of his honour many a generation
    murmurs
Because of him girls studying philosophy become numb with fear
And during crazy spring days the room smells of hemlock
Oh to render judgement on oneself, oh to cut off one's own head
In special moments it becomes clear – we should talk of pigs
They have not met their own death proudly
From the early morning they weep in their slums at the end of town
Tears stream down their pink snouts
Fear flows in their veins, it's wartime
And the time has come for us to finally start talking of pigs
Scorn was the prophet's punishment, they wallow in mud dreaming
Of a deep clear lake, pines rustling in the morning, glacier peaks
Perhaps, childhood scenes in the distance. Pigs bid farewell to
    everything
While muddy with shame they receive their last supper
Nobody is going to meet them in the afterlife
History textbooks will absorb all their blood
And nothing will remain, not even a printing error, a hand quiver
    on the paper,
Or their tears. At least that much has been left after socrates
Therefore in those special moments let us close our eyes and start
    talking of pigs.

MILJENKO JERGOVIĆ
Bosnia / Zagreb
Translated by Mario Suško

The Scaffold

for me it's easy

with an eternal smile I put my head on the block
can't say if somewhere else something harder than life awaits me
but the executioner has to raise the heavy axe
and look me straight in the eyes

why did he stop

what did he see in my eye – in a green mirror

this:
there's an executioner above him raising an axe
and an executioner above that executioner
and an executioner above that executioner
and an executioner above that executioner...

and another and another interminably

believe me it's easy for me

with an eternal smile I put my head on the block
can't say if somewhere else something harder than life awaits me
but the executioner has to raise the heavy axe
and look me straight in the eyes

straight in the eyes

JOSIP OSTI
Bosnia / Ljubljana
Translated by Mario Suško

The Mickey-Mouse Gas Mask

In the country of comparative peace,
conscious of trees, I taste my far-from-clear
citizenship: like continental mourning kept
in an Italian hurtwood marriage-chest.

I have never been out in so black a night,
people stood in the roped-off streets
watching the sky.
The Clubhouse's pretty double-drawing room
had gone completely flat, its back
as if a giant knife had cut it through.
Huge blocks of stone were thrown up in the air
like cricket balls, furnishings were flung
fifty yards on to the course. Every window
missing, the church had only its spire left.

This war of movement seems to travel
like a reverse letter 'L', the long arm
loaded with Maid-of-Honour cakes. The other
a dog-photographer's water-only meal.

MEDBH McGUCKIAN
Belfast

The Light

He slips it in sheathing it almost
too easily on the sluice of his comrades.
At the end of the day there's time to think
through the rhythm how easily

things slip in – the bayonet
between the third and fourth ribs, the canister
into the breach, the shells into the heart
of the queue in the city below scattering
bread everywhere, how easily
he's slipped into manhood

and learned this rhythm. No doubt
slips in except at the peak: Why
won't she look at him taking note
in the lull to ask the old sergeant unsheathing it
and slipping into the night, her eyes

circling wildly round his back remembering
her mother's last words before she slipped
into madness – when the light
is too bright look around all around look everywhere else
but directly at it.

JEFFREY LEE SCHNEIDER
Ellenville, New York

Frontier

Summer's hot on the Hron delta. This border village
where storks return each year from nobler eons
before border guards, central planning
or Velveeta Revolutions.

They look ironic with their long beaks
on the fertile *planina*. They carry no passports
across hollow lobbies of territory
but go where they will.

A man in Bosnia calls his enemies 'cabbage'.
The storks fly over Austerlitz, Ypres and Normandy,
where young men once lay torn.

They too abhor these trigger-happy morons
itching to relieve their inner doubt
with blasts of red. Hungary glares at Slovakia,
a way line on a map, a treaty

signed by ghosts. Soldiers stalk the narrow lanes of wrath.
Soar home, storks –
leave them where they belong.

TOM REYNOLDS
Sberomova, Slovakia

It Was Ever Thus

There's a lot of guys making a lot
of money out of this war, for if
they weren't, there wouldn't be
any war.

IVOR CUTLER
London

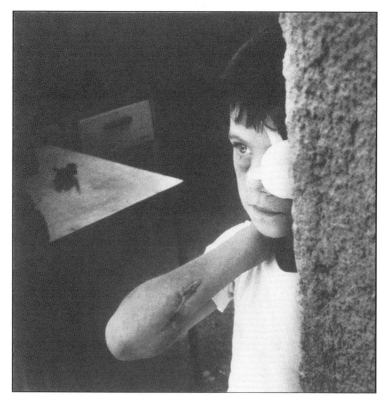

EDHEM DEDOVIC, 11, WOUNDED IN A MORTAR ATTACK AND BLINDED IN ONE EYE,
PICTURED 16 AUGUST 1993 BEFORE EVACUATION TO THE UK.

[Untitled]

25 May 1993: Bosko Brokić (Serb) and Admira Ismić (Muslim),
both 25, sweethearts since childhood, shot dead trying to escape
from Sarajevo, their home town. Both sides deny responsibility.
Their bodies lay five days in no man's land, unclaimed.

The beauty of flesh
hands on each other's bodies
nipples that bloom like plums
your prick a root planted within me

The fragility of flesh
shrapnel that peels the skin
eyes exploding like orchids
your love not enough to save me

SUSAN BASSNETT
Leicestershire

Love Story, Bosnia
i.m. Bosko Brokić and Admira Ismić

Bosko and Admira
huddle near in no-man's-land,
hand almost touching hand.
They do not move as other lovers.

Dead cellars of Sarajevo.
Birds beat on the empty wind.
Playground silence broken
by the cackle of assault rifles.

The sweater his mother knitted for her
lies on the grave her mother cannot visit.

Helpless as words,
their few flowers wilt in the indifferent sun.

ADRIAN HENRI
Liverpool

Safe Haven

An air raid shelter
down in the street.
Packed, and somebody chucked
a grenade inside it.

A solidly logical
construction. Walls and roof
kept faith,
with never a crack.

That's proof
if you like.
And once hosed out
can be used again and again.

G.F. DUTTON
Perthshire

The Blind Eye

the blind eye
turned in
gawping
through cracks
in the heart

JENNIE FONTANA
Brighton

Sergeant, A Company, First Battalion

The soldier's name has not yet been released.

When mortar shells banged closer through that night,
With you on guard and writing home to me
You managed, still, to joke about the light
You wanted out. I read that 'half-past-three'
And wondered just what time the firing ceased

In Bosnian dark. I added to my list
Of close escapes I think I know you've had:
The mine which rings your ears; the shots which missed
But rattled hard across your turret lid;

Your stumble down that cliff on mud and grease;
'The tell-tale whistle of artillery';
...*a Warrior Commander badly shot*...
Then silence. No news further reaches me.
I hope it's you they've wounded, hope it's not.

The soldier's name has not yet been released.

DAVID HUGHES
York

Refugees

In dusk of helmet brims the eyes look stern,
Unwavering; no matter what they see
Or where they gaze – Bluff Cove, Thermopylae,
Kuwait, The Somme – the pillaged cities burn,
And when the owners of those eyes return
And put away their weapons there will be
An alien music in a harsher key,
New words and syntax difficult to learn.

Wars never end. Across the livid plain
The dark processions trail, the refugees,
Anonymous beneath indifferent skies,
Somnambulistic, patient shapes of pain,
Long commentary on war, an ancient frieze
Of figures we refuse to recognise.

VERNON SCANNELL
Otley, West Yorkshire

Nocturne

They are skinning the land with hoes
and picks, and the broken teeth
of Muslim girls; after they've buggered them
once or twice – for a laugh.
The Nocturnes of Chopin
settle like flies on the tablecloth.
Something is wrong: the piano
is out of tune. Either that
or I've forgotten how to listen any more.

The Elected Representatives
are breakfasting on Balkan prawns:
and very nice they are too.
They are having a meeting
to decide the time and place
of the next meeting.
A hundred thousand dead
and what shall we do?

If I pull this line between my fingers
the whole palm will unravel.
'Hold out your hand,' she says;
and with a fingernail
painted in Burgundy, she traces the boundaries
of 20th century Europe.
'Here is the Kaiser's hat;
here is Stalin's moustache,' she says.
'Here is your mother digging a hole,
here is the sweat on her head.
You can't see a single thing can you?'

NEIL ROLLINSON
Bath

From the hills, the town

As he talks he rolls an apple in his hands
which with the force of his thumbs
he splits to make two glistening
full-waxed moons of sweet flesh.
Below, the town is a mouth of broken teeth.
In his mind it is geometry, lines form a grid
– the runway, the mosques, the bread shops.
His face is a map of the long year.

Stones and mortars. But now it is a quiet time.
Though the day still has warmth, his men huddle
around a stove, the smoke of bacon, coffee.
Suddenly hungry, his eyes blink wide.
He fits the two apple halves back together
and bites from one, then the other.

TONY CURTIS
Barry, Glamorgan

Night Patrol

What is there on a deep night in August
That conspires to lay a simple trap
Of moonlight, an empty road, a forest?
Why must a soldier guard his moving thought
Against conceit or against emptying
Into the imagined a last bullet?

The heavy insects knock against the wood
Of his gun as though in the instrument
Of death there is always a hidden light.
Behind a thicket the noctural beast
Drinks from its own shadowy reflection,
Its nostrils quivering at the coolness.

At each step he takes the soldier creates
A pocket of sound, a barren crater
Into which dust, pebble and stone spill back
As if to say, *Who makes the silences?*
Who is architect to these silences,
To all silence, if not a silent god?

The beast lifts its shadow from the water.
Listens. A ripple spreads along its flank
And through the fabric of all that listens.
The smooth leaf parts company with the branch,
And the owl blinks. The bearer of the gun
Absorbs through his body a disturbed earth.

MARIUS KOCIEJOWSKI
London

A Dog's Life in Bosnia

Our home mortgaged to fear,
when I looked at the coffee-pot,
the dog's scratch marks on doors,
they weren't real, we'd lost
the right to ourselves.

Enemies held the key.
The children asked and asked
and I had no answers, tried
to play games
and lost every round.

I begged him to leave,
I knew he should. But nights,
together I was alone but still
alive. They came, of course,
took him outside...

We couldn't move for hours,
days. Then I made food,
held on to the children, afraid
to look in their eyes. I still am.
When friends came to help

I went outside to find him.
Then understood why the dog
had not been hungry. How
can I live? Why do you ask me
questions? I have no answers.

ANNE BORN
Salcombe, Devon

Recipe for Saving the World

In the manufacturing shops of Kraus Maffay
and Royal Ordnance a rusty wind will blow
through the assembly lines
when fruit suddenly rules the earth.

The EC ministers will agree for the first time:
Watermelons as ammunition for Croat tanks,
grapes and pineapples as weapons
for Serb besiegers, bananas for the snipers.

Nothing but kiwis would be smuggled across the Danube
in the hollow bellies of barges. The U.N.
could decide on kumquat embargos, order peace keepers
to train in the disarming of oranges.

The worst scenario would be huge fruit salads
in the streets of Mostar, where the children
in hospital would complain about stomach upsets
and vitamin shocks.

Tangerine futures would keep stock brokers
on their toes, borders would remain untouched even
by peach skirmishes. Heads of government would now
become suspect for their strawberry affairs.

I for one have planted my apple tree.

KATJA WESSELS
Berlin
Translated from the German by Margitt Lehbert

Getting up in Arms

We sat round the table arguing
and demonstrating – like old colonels –
by manoeuvring the butter dish, the knives.

The air-strike supporters
were at odds with the pacifists.
The timbre of voices coarsened;

sudden rifts appeared in old
friendships. The humanitarian-aid-only
contingent banged the table.

Our waiter, clearing away the ruins
of the meal asked us
What are you fighting about?

CONNIE BENSLEY
London

Flying the Flag in Bosnia

Her face is hidden by her hands,
But the hands are enough.
She is slumped by the cross
Which bears her son's name,
Crudely lettered.
An old woman
Whose hair is parted
Straight down the middle.
On one arm of the cross
Some keys and a wallet.
Below, between two lighted candles,
A full cup of coffee,
Left by the grave digger.
Draped on the cross
A shirt, almost new,
Creases still crisp from the iron,
Is unfurled by the wind
Like a flag,
In a country which already has
Too many.

DEREK POWER
Taunton

Leave the Window Open

Leave the window open leave the window
for the air of the street to come let it all burn out

Leave the window open leave the window
to swallow up breath to let out the odour of the body

Leave the window open leave the window
to break the vision in the eyes to clarify the spirit
from the closed space

Leave the window open leave the window
resounds the epic voice of the poets children rush to
escape from darkness from the sharpened tones

Leave the window open leave the window
the beasts come down the mountains they thread upon the apples
in dead women

Leave the window open leave the window
it rains water some water especially some water drop
on the chopped lips

Leave the window open leave the window
free yourself of passion of guilt greet your dead especially

Leave the window open leave the window
sleep with dogs insects with spirits of the dark
with faraway voices

Leave the window open leave the window
corpses are your sincere companions, look they do not kill you
do not stand on your way do not take your breath

Leave the window open leave the window
red rain drops before you are off in that final journey
with umbrellas of steel

Leave the window open leave the window
break the quadratic mirror in the corner of the room
with your face and set off

Leave the window open leave the window especially
as you are dead in the army marching to the heavens
close the door close
lest the beasts and humans get out

BASRI ÇAPRIQI
Kosovo, Serbia / London

The Skeleton in the Cupboard

is coiled in, wound like a snake in a spiral
of its spine, the knobbed beads of the vertebrae
balancing one on another, resting, embracing,
intimate as one woman's hands colliding quietly,
unsure which palm is touching, which is touched,
whether fingers of dexter or sinister take the lead.

It is one woman infinitely elongated in the dark
like the life of Woolf's Orlando stretched as a drumskin
on the centuries; this time she's skinless as a stone
or as strung stones in an endless necklace
looped carefully on itself in the cupboard they tried
to forget and papered over with a flower design.

Oh the long drip of phalanges into stalactites behind
the door, the bleaching of repeated knucklebones
where they hang then fold onto the floor; she grows
new small joints as years fade the covering paper,
fails to dwindle away, pressing those concentric rings
of her ribs into corners that remembering had left empty.

ANNEMARIE AUSTIN
Weston-super-Mare

Sentence

The dress you burnt to burn his smell:
the dress you'll wear

under your skin
for the rest of your life –

where it rots – this
foul cocoon of charred grave-clothes.

TONY FLYNN
Walsall

Historic Winter

december 1956
wörgl in austria

there are frosted planks on a lorry
I load them on to a railway-truck at the station
and buy rilke's selected poems out of my wages

so as to warm me up

december 1992
sarajevo
r.l. a bosnian poet feeds a fire with his rilke

to keep from freezing to death

ELEMÉR HORVÁTH
Hungary / USA
Translated from the Hungarian by Clive Wilmer & George Gömöri

Hand-Me-Downs

The nineteenth century of the bizarre
system of dates the Christians have
stands almost empty. Everybody
who helped design the first of the World
Wars is dead, no longer doing much
to anybody; likewise most of the begetters
and settlers-up of the next. They've got
clean away. And so on.

Turnips, four short rows, but enough.
Potatoes, plenty. Kale. For surplus
baby tomatoes, a jar with olive oil
an inch deep over the fruit,
then topped off with aqua vitae,
to rest on the oil and guard it. And
seal tight. And look forward
to winter. Ordinary life,
'restorable' 'normal' 'life' – paraffin,
pepper, fingers that stroke and grip –
sits in the brain like the supreme contemptuous
coinage of disease, nothing more
than a counter devised for murderers to bargain with.

ROY FISHER
Buxton

Bogomil in Languedoc

One stone at Domazan is enough.
In southern France among
the Catharist sarcophagi beyond
a village full of tiled roofs.

He is the warrior of Radimlja and he
has come this far. He raises both his arms.
He spreads wide both enormous hands.
Although he is entirely silent here,

his mason, up from Tuscany and
proselytizing slogs along the hot Apennine,
spouted bits he'd learned from
Interrogatio Johannis to his missionary

friend who left the book at Carcassonne.
When all matter is to be destroyed,
the stone warrior here at Domazan
will give the sign. He will finally

drop his arms. And where he stood
the hole in space will spread until
all nothing speaks in tongues to no one.
May he, then, forever raise his hands.

JOHN MATTHIAS
South Bend, Indiana

In Moslodina

If we never learn much from history
it is because 'we' are always different people.

In the Grand Hotel somebody leaves a tap
Running too long. The first drip to drop on me
Strikes at my left thigh. The second stays
Poised over the armchair, then suddenly
Runs, and falls several inches farther up.
The third and fourth I catch in two ashtrays.

Forgetting my own bath, I rush to get
Dressed and raise Cain, cursing a world with too
Many forgetful fools in it, surely far
More than there used to be? Plus, a huge new
Tribe of the unknowing, happy to let
Some others tell them what their memories are.

The drips fill tumblers, vases. Through the dead
Door of the room upstairs a national song
Booms, to drown my knocking. Girls in folkloric dress
Light candles on TV... I watch a long
Dark, cross-shaped patch on the ceiling form, and spread:
A continent of sheer forgetfulness.

ALAN BROWNJOHN
London

Sarajevo

Now that a revolution really is needed, those who once were fervent, are quite cool.

While a country, murdered and raped, calls for help from the Europe which it had trusted, they yawn.

While statesmen choose villainy and no voice is raised to call it by name.

The rebellion of the young who called for a new earth was a sham, and that generation has written the verdict on itself.

Listening with indifference to the cries of those who perish because they are just barbarians killing each other

And the lives of the well-fed are worth more than the lives of the starving.

It is revealed now that their Europe since the beginning has been a deception, for its foundation is nothingness.

Nothingness, as the prophets keep saying, brings forth only nothingness and they will be led once again like cattle to slaughter.

Let them tremble and at the last moment comprehend that the word Sarajevo will from now on mean the destruction of their sons and the debasement of their daughters.

They prepare it by repeating: 'We at least are safe,' unaware that what will strike ripens in themselves.

CZESLAW MILOSZ
Berkeley, California
Translated from the Polish by the author and Robert Hass

The Encounter

They are there side by side: the familiar and the unthinkable;
An Elton John T-shirt blowing on a clothes line;
A young mother in a kitchen being raped on the table.

Later she would say, 'He had an ear-ring in one ear.'
And then, after a silence. 'The day he first wore it
He came round to show us. He was only a teenager.'

She flattened her hand and brought it sharply to her face,
'And then it was this close. It was almost in my mouth.'
A sudden catching of her breath. 'How can they do this?'

In the field above her house we looked down on the village.
Now it was almost evening and a light wind was blowing.
The red roofs of the houses had buckled like bridges.

I saw her in silhouette. Eventually she started speaking.
'I once stood here for pleasure. When I look now at those houses,
At those craters in the road we used to cycle down each morning,

I see how our memories, or the places they depend on,
Are also being destroyed. And so sometimes I imagine
That our past is withdrawing and leaving us on a thin line

Between no past and no future. Do you understand what I mean?'
The wind was getting up. I nodded and we walked on.
At the cross-roads we parted and she walked down the lane.

SIMON RICHEY
London

do dh'ioslamaich bosnia, bliadhna mhath ùr, 1993

ged a tha brùid air do dhruim
a drùdhadh ort le buillean
(sinne 'ga fhaicinn)
ged a sgàineadh e do mhnathan –
a bhrùid againne th'ann

cobhair? nam b'urrainn dhuinn –

cha b'e d'fhuil, cha b'e d'innleachd
ach gu faic sinn
luibhe choimheach na do chridhe –

lethsgial nach aidich sinn...

to the muslims of bosnia, a happy new year, 1993

though there's a brute on your back
sapping you with blows
(while we observe)
though he'd rip   your women apart –
he's *our* brute

help? If only we could –

it's not your blood, or your deeds
but that we can see
a foreign weed in your heart –

the excuse we won't declare...

AONGHAS MACNEACAIL
Edinburgh

44

The Ghosts Return

What we did was simple,
we saw the things to hate,
the people to make scapegoats,
the way geography was used
to trick us, stories history told
to hold us back – not only did
we have no need of secrets
we saw how populations hate
complexity; we were pioneers
of the easily felt, conduits
of the bile which numbers
and despair impose on everyone;
our urgent plans expanded
on red horizons, our lack of jokes
brought the roof of Heaven down
on caterwauling prophets.

Now from our proper hells
we look in wonder at
the explanations of our heirs,
their armoury of paradox
designed to hold off guilt,
above all we are mystified
by their pose of understanding –
the early wars, the brutal
acts of union, set against
a pious care for poverty,
state safety nets and subsidies,
the frequent festivals.
We rise from our oblivion –
we ask for balconies to speak from,
a square to take salute in –
people are waiting to be told
whose fault it is, watching
for the star of destiny, a sign
to follow to another birth.

PETER PORTER
London

Bosnia Tune

As you sip your brand of scotch,
crush a roach or scratch your crotch,
as your hand adjusts your tie,
people die.

In the towns with funny names,
hit by bullets, caught in flames,
by and large, not knowing why,
people die.

In small places you don't know
of, yet big for having no
chance to scream or say goodbye,
people die.

People die as you elect
new apostles of neglect,
self-restraint, etc – whereby
people die.

Too far off to practise love
for thy neighbour/brother Slav,
where our cherubs dread to fly,
people die.

As you watch the athletes score,
check your latest statement, or
kissing your child a lullaby,
people die.

Time, whose sharp, blood-thirsty quill
parts the killed from those who kill,
will pronounce the latter tribe
as your type.

JOSEPH BRODSKY
New York

Food for the Dead

In some parts of Europe still
it's the custom to feed the dead –
the dead man's favourite dishes
in a pot or canister or simply on a plate
are set beside the grave
It is summer 1990   Once again
a restless early summer now
and a spectacular feeding time for the dead
the erstwhile Titan of the Carpathians eats his fill
of the young   their flesh   their broken bones
and then instead of a brandy he slurps at
gypsy blood and the blood of bearded protesters
he keeps coming back from the grave   snarling
a black zombie hoarsely demanding: Food
more food more of it let me eat

GEORGE GÖMÖRI
Cambridge
Translated from the Hungarian by the author and Clive Wilmer

Horror

Broken streets. Broken footsteps.
Broken cages for birds and animals called – people
Broken youths in broken cars
Broken skulls in broken hospitals
Broken brains on broken tables
Broken girlish giggles in a broken cellar
Broken foetuses in broken wombs
Broken mothers on broken burial mounds
Broken breath in the broken government air
Broken heart on the broken threshold
Broken thoughts in broken dustbins
Broken God in his broken temple
Broken earth under the broken cupola of heaven
Broken self.

Smashed skulls on smashed spines
Smashed clavicle
Smashed pelvic bone on the woman who just gave birth
Smashed young bones in young flesh
Smashed bullets by a smashed wall
Smashed vowels in smashed exhalations
Smashed child's knee on the smashed arm of his father
Smashed instruments in the smashed hands of the doctor
Smashed rose petals in smashed garden ornaments
Smashed prayers in smashed tongues
Smashed self.

Frightened beasts in their frightened lairs
Frightened children in frightened games
Frightened shoppers for bread in the frightened square
Frightened passengers on the frightened bus
Frightened voices of speakers on the frightened news
Frightened candles in frightened cellars
Frightened lungs in the frightened air
Frightened blossom on the frightened branches
Frightened soldiers, frightened guns at the ready
Frightened citizens in frightened offices
Frightened articles in frightened newspapers
Frightened voices of relatives in frightened neighbouring countries

Frightened water in the kettle in the frightened evenings
Frightened anaesthetics in frightened glass cupboards
Frightened backs under frightened cudgels
Frightened vagina of a frightened schoolgirl
Frightened souls cowering in frightened flesh
Frightened self.

STEVAN TONTIĆ
Sarajevo / Berlin
Translated from the Serbian by Mary Radosavljević

from Joe Soap

O and one more thing:
from the rubble of a dead bungalow a father
wearing a blood-shadow on his jersey.
    Don't ask me how it got there.

O and one more thing:
in the dawn smoke of a bare street a soldier
heaving a black plastic bag which still twitches.
    Don't ask me what is in there.

O and one more thing:
beneath the skin of the harbour basin a wound
leaking pus which boils when it meets the surface.
    Don't ask me what goes on there.

O and one more thing:
on the wind through the whole city a blizzard
of human cinders which are warm and taste sweet.
    Don't ask me how to live there.

ANDREW MOTION
London

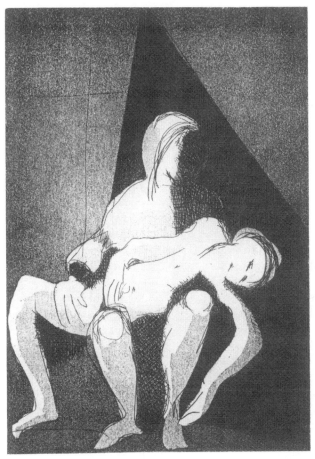

Pietà in spitbite

eye and socket; the
exit wound of the bullet
the mark and the void

PAULINE STAINER
Dunmow, Essex

Essential Serbo-Croat

Guraj	Push
Pomozi mi	Help me
Boli	It hurts
Boli me	I have a pain
Boli me ovdje	I have a pain here
Bole me grudi	I have a pain in my breast
Bole me prsa	I have a pain in my chest
Boli me oko	I have a pain in my eye
Boli me stopalo	I have a pain in my foot
Boli me glava	I have a pain in my head
Hitno je	It's urgent
Ozbiljno je	It's serious
Boli me ovdje	It hurts here
Boli puno	It hurts a lot
To je jaka bol	It's a sharp pain
To je mrtva bol	It's a dull pain
To je uporna bol	It's a nagging pain
Vecinom vremena	Most of the time
Vrti mi se u glavi	I feel dizzy
Zlo mi je	I feel sick
Slabo mi je	I feel weak
Nije dobro	It's no good
Izgubio sam sve	I have lost everything
Ne mogu vam pomoci	I can't help you

KEN SMITH
London

Big Shifts

The coast's magenta. There's a yellow hut
couched on the sands in a reality
translated out of Paul Klee's small harbour,

no swimmers anywhere, the sea
an oyster coloured watered-silk. 'It's ten
o'clock,' he says, 'in any century,
not mine, not yours,' and she looks into space,
expecting clock hands on the sun,
the punctual aircraft to arrive,
bringing them news of how the others live
in Yellow Chasm, Diamond Falls, Sirocco Road.

They pick up starfish, a folded *Le Monde*
used as a prop for a sunbather's head.
The date's been bleached out by the sun.
That was when people read the days
as continuity. They sit and wait:

she eats a yellow pear, watches him swim,
and anyhow the plane is late.

JEREMY REED
London

Recalling Former Travels: Yugoslavia '72

At first light we wake
to find four pears on a nest
of brown paper damp with dew.
They hold the thick green light
of morning, their bruises
richly metallic in the shadow
of the tent. A couple slump
against each other – nature
morte – and I feel the light
presence still of the hands
that have borne them, laid them
down so gently the grass stems
barely bend. Skin, flesh
and core – we eat the lot.
But sweet as they were
if you showed me a map
or took me to the spot,
I fear I'd never again find
the village where once
they spoke with such eloquence
the ripe language of pears.

TOM POW
Dumfries

Foreign Travel

It could have been France or at a pinch England.
Wet all over the hills. A lot of grey stone and clouds
and hardly any buses. It was difficult for us,
waiting amid the rain for buses,
and for whatever else we wanted to stop or start,
to happen or not happen.
Hard grey beds in the one star hotels.

Once by a bus-stop,
a rustle in the wet leaves. A grasshopper,
as big and as complicated as a Swiss Army knife,
though green of course, clambering
stiffly. Once at the bottom of a culverted river,
a snake, flat on the hard grey bed; winding slowly,
raising a cloudy track. Following a private need,
or perhaps even drowning.

You've seen those bands of young men;
musical bands, with drums and trumpets?
Did you ever see one *disband*? To silence,
and then fragment into red-cheeked louts,
pulling out their fags in relief
from shiny harmony? There was that, too.
It fitted somewhat. No chance
of my seeing that country again.

TED BURFORD
London

55

Old Sarajevo

i.m. Graham Bamford

Talk of Bosnia; a table loaded with bottles.
The Irish for *minaret, solar plexus?*

Is this the unrhapsodised gloss on Achilles,
burnt limewash and *súgán*, a tidal wave of killings?

Hale fellows make a *teach-an-asal* of cabbage beds.
Cashel's turfsmoke twisting and a spit in the wind.

Old Sarajevo! Tomorrow, the Shell-pump's sunny vista.
Past *cré na cille* the living debate the dead.

CHRIS AGEE
Belfast

Graham Bamford immolated himself in front of the Houses of Parliament in
protest against British policy in Bosnia. Cashel is a small Irish-speaking town-
land in the West of Ireland. *Súgán*: rope used in thatching. *Teach-an-asal*: an
idiom for toilet. *Cré na cille*: a churchyard.

Waiting in Macedonia

In an empty hotel on the border
Of a country with no army,
The rooms shuttered, the pool
Given over to mosquitoes,
Children playing with bank-notes,
Furtive adults hoarding petrol,
The coco-cola signs, the travel adverts,
Kitsch exhibits from a museum now.
Down in the town the side-walk cafés
Bubble with rumours. Like clothes
That have been locked away too long,
Old prejudices aired.
Someone mentions the British,
Someone mentions the Greeks,
Someone mentions the Albanians.
Someone admits they don't understand.
Someone orders a coffee and a doughnut,
And whistles after a pretty girl who is passing.

BRIAN PATTEN
London

Bosnian
(Sarajevo, 1992)

Sipping grit-coffee and vinjak outside a
    bar in the Turkish
Quarter, observe how Hooded Crows crowd and
    bicker for carrion
in the fast-darkening air grown rank with
    barbecued lambs' smoke.

PETER READING
Melbourne, Australia

Peace Memories of Sarajevo

Sarajevo glowing white
as a translucent china cup

Sarajevo forty poets in suits on an official platform
Reciting eight lines each under a giant portrait of Tito

Sarajevo my daughter aged eight laughing
As she stands in the concrete rain-filled footsteps
Of Avril the assassin

Sarajevo in the smoky little orchards on the hills
Families sitting under gentle-eyed blossoms
Enjoying their slow dinners

Sarajevo and my brave schoolmaster friend
Who did not blink when the bureaucrats spat in his eye

Sarajevo I wish you no bombs no shells no guns
I wish you smoky little orchards and glowing poets
And soldiers who refuse to kill
And children who refuse to kill

And Sarajevo
Glowing white
As a translucent china cup

ADRIAN MITCHELL
London

Rosa Rasandić, 1962

Bumpy journey down the Dalmatian coast
of Yugoslavia, but a lot of friendliness.
'Communism *works* here,' we said as we washed
at the village tap in Podgora and cleaned our teeth.
A widow beckoned us into her cave-like house –
Rosa Rasandić. She knew a little English;
offered us slivovitz, bread, olives, grapes,
was self-sufficient. It was an earthquake
that had cracked her walls and killed her husband
five months back, but she wasn't short of much.
Her donkey was cropping a little patch of grass.
Once, she said, she'd been to Sarajevo
where her son lived. ('Big, big city – and shops!')
'All Bosna-i-Hercegovina is good place.
Here earthquakes only thing we are afraid of.'
I often think of Rosa Rasandić, in black,
who had journeyed to Sarajevo once
and thanked God her grandchildren were safe for life.

SYLVIA KANTARIS
Helston, Cornwall

War and Peace

The woods of Normandy are hot with stars
underfoot, resistance and memory.
It's the Queen's birthday and we know the stars
are flowers in reality because
today flowers are everywhere for her.
Yellow smoke hangs over the bridge
at Mostar and someone has taken
huge bites out of the town, chewed up
roads, apartment blocks. It's peaceful.

Even the mourners at a country wake
break off at three to sing 'Happy birthday Queen'
and catching themselves solemn for no good reason
crack up with a laughter that makes tears run.
And why not, I say, give to the dead the giggles
you normally would squander on the living?
Yes, it's peacetime. Grab your shopping trolley
at Tesco's and read the sign: 'Do not hesitate
when passing through this gate'

and you don't, you don't hesitate
knowing you're about to buy a world
in the supermarket someone else lost recently.
Peacetime. Here is Mostar still dressed
in yellow smoke. The Queen marks her anniversary
by doing a bungee jump at Crystal Palace –
a two hundred foot plunge in full regalia.
She yo-yos up and down as her tiara
crashes to the ground. A mess of yellow clouds

passes behind the roof of the chateau,
windows and their frames are blown out
and works of art are moved elsewhere.
The problem is not living together, pulling together,
the problem is dying. A little boat
leaves the bridge at Mostar and shudders
towards the white mists of Niagara,
whose plunge and roar is thrilling all the tourists.

Peace. The engines grind against the undertow
as the captain takes us as far into the mist
and thunder as he thinks we dare to go.

JO SHAPCOTT
London

Disturbing Images

A three-ring circus: Bosnian, Croat, Serb.
Joy-riding cars that careless mount the kerb.

Black comedy: promises from dark suits.
Hot speeches about 'cleansing', 'faith', and 'roots'.

Block-headed huge commanders with the guns.
Cutting of throats for mothers, daughters, sons.

The tortures come in many shapes and sizes.
The newest and the best might well win prizes.

GAVIN EWART
London

Song of a Survivor

This country weighs so heavy
Sometimes I cannot breathe
Under each rock, a skull
Under the plough, teeth
In every village graveyard
Names of slaughtered brothers
Who fell against each other
Till fish in lakes and sea
Grew fat on their corpses
And in every river, blood

How many more centuries
To ease the wails of mothers
Scratched in walls of farms
And hanging from barn rafters
How long before revenge
Dies in its own bath
Before the clansmen forget
Their enemies' grandchildren
And sharpening of knives
In long awaited ambush

And yet, hard, rugged land
Merciless, wild, ravaged
You have showered beauty on me
To bandage up my nightmares
Nourished me with your love
Filled my palms with bread
And salt, into my mouth
Poured dark wine and kisses
And, gazing through open eyes
Taught me to fear nothing.

RICHARD BURNS
Cambridge

Bosnia Festival:
Your Full Guide by Our Arts Reporter

At 10.00 a.m., mime show
by The Shuffling Headscarves.
Nothing much happens;
some shuffling, weeping.
Mimed weeping, that is.

At Midday, cabaret
in The Bread Queue
by The Arguing Headscarves.
Nothing much happens;
a feeble argument. Behind them
The Ducking Headscarves
are ducking the snipers.
The Shuffling Headscarves
mime weeping.

At Three P.M. a one man show
by a man in a white suit
talking into a camera.
Nothing much happens.
The Shuffling Headscarves, The
Arguing Headscarves and the Ducking
Headscarves continue their act

which one critic described
as a lot of shuffling, arguing
and ducking.

There's so much happening.
There's almost too much to take in.
A kind of festival fatigue
comes over you: all these headscarves,
all that weeping, all those gestures.

Godot turned up last night, by the way,
in a headscarf, weeping.

The actors stood with their mouths open
like fish. Fish on a bloody slab.

IAN McMILLAN
Barnsley

John Bosnia

We have the biggest mushrooms in the world.
If you are lucky enough to collect a basketful,
Take them home & cook them.
Wait a year or so. If you're still alive
Buy some more & try again. Either way
The process is definitive.
Then we have Hercegovina, which means (roughly),
The Prince Who Drank (And Keeps Drinking) (And Is
                    In A Perpetual State Of Drinking)
The Wine. We call this the continual case
Which does not exist in yr language. Yet.
Climb our many mountains, you will see a shepherd descending.
For *dvije banke* he will sell you the body
Of his goat. We are hard people. We take our pleasure fiercely.
Someone told me to ask an Englishman
To write this down on paper for me. Is this word 'fiercely' correct?
It sounds funny.
I have been ejected from more restaurants
                            in yr country than in any other.
Our waiters are not like yours. They are very male. They are
                            not embarassed to embrace you,
Press their moustaches against yr ear & tell you to leave,
Whilst holding yr waist in a tight grip.
It feels very unusual, but Englishmen think it more direct & honest
And grow to like it. And if you can
Wrestle the bloomers off the swarthy women of my country
You've had it, my friend, you're done for. When a Bosnian woman
Presses you to eat, you may not rise from the table
Until you are dead with exhaustion. You must experience
What it means to go beyond gratification.
Then you will understand. Ah, we are too patriotic, I know,
And when we kiss
Often it is kinder to put a knife in someone's ribs. But we are very
        gentle people.
We have the biggest mosquitoes.
Strangely, the nights here are vacant of whine. How do you sleep?
I was caught in a storm
Driving my melons to market. The old horse skipped a little

And then fell into the Drina, turning it red. All
The opened faces of the melons began to talk in prophecies. They
     said:
Stand up & go to London. Ask an Englishman to write this down:
'My name's John Bosnia, I have lost my cart & my crop,
And before you throw me out of this restaurant
I am going to read you this poem.'

JOHN HARTLEY WILLIAMS
Berlin

A Basket of Dalmatian Oysters
i.m. Hubert Butler

1

When I visited him in his office
I saw on his desk what I took to be
a basket of shelled Dalmatian oysters.
'A gift from my Bosnian Ustashe,'
he smiled. I looked closer and they were eyes.

2

You drink with them carafes of rakkia
and look for the forgiving among folk
in black for the Battle of Kosovo,
1389, year of the young Turk.
Like us, they ask about America.

IAN DUHIG
Leeds

The Search for Scarlett

Not one yet
among all these so sharp with want
so many so many and wrong
yet she exists, somewhere,
she is Tess among the sheaves she is
rising in Africa her eyes bolts
out of the blue the dune hides her
she is in the street in Stockholm
she turns on her blond heel at the next corner
she is in school, pouting with boredom
her mouth forms over the pencil
a lovely O
O she is there all right she is
superb, undeniable, when she walks
into the studio they will all shut up
aghast all these gaunt girls
everyone will know her
she will not walk into the studio
she is in Russia
she has a rough cape over her shoulder
she is hidden in Dublin, she is not old enough
wait two years and she will burn
with her two red cheeks and two round breasts
she is learning in a back road in Cambodia her family
will send her into the city she will send them money
they know her worth she is in a library
in Boston and has not yet considered
this seriously she is serious she wipes her glasses
and looks blurredly past her thick lashes
her hair is Gaelic she is getting out of the Shetlands
it clouds her she twists it back she struts
to the bus-stop her clothes are all wrong
but all right anyway it's the way
of her it's Central America
she is going to die before she makes it
it's Sarajevo
Sarajevo says my printer over and over
printing out poems its lights squeeze open and shut

the lights have another purpose she is mute
she is Muslim the child she will bear
is a Serb if it lives
she flings her look she is in a cave
she is under a bridge she is afraid
of an aeroplane
she is laughing the big moon
smooths her big limbs she has lost Tara
Tara of the plains Tara of the sandbank
Tara of the terrible southern marshes
Tara of the city
she has no substitute
she will be difficult to locate
she is probably black
she is not a pretender
you have to go to her
she will not come, search on she is some
where

HEATHER SPEARS
Canada / Copenhagen

Spectators and Protagonists

if i am to come back, like an ant,
with a dry leaf of grass,
to be part of moving, could live through the winter –
prove my sense of bearings,

if through a magnifying glass i'm watched
by an expert who measures my habits
creates artificial obstacles and places
more fancifully coloured plastic straw pieces

O, reason,
if i know that all this is some stage
i'll be lifted carefully from with tweezers
and pinned on a tray once and for all –
like that one chasing the girl across the urn

(if nothing else they will not mark my leg
i'll sit behind the glass
grinning at anyone watching the unusual specimen
a remarkable intelligence that only
a proportion prevents to start a revolution
topple the natural order and send everything into mother energy) –

MARIO SUŠKO
Sarajevo / Norwich
Translated by Mario Suško

For Bosnia

The Bogomils
may well have been
Beloved of God

but they were despised
by Rome and Byzantium
for their silly heresy
of God and Satan
slugging it out like wrestlers

till the Turks arrived
and far from resisting
like decent Christian folk

they embraced the conquerors
put on their titles
their baggy trousers
became Slavs more Ottoman
than the Ottoman

and sent the sons
of poor Christians
to war for Islam.

All that is left
of the Bogomils
are crudely carved
gravestones depicting
men with hands held high

like those on newsreels
from a nation whose
memory is too long.

KEITH BOSLEY
Slough

Again

If I have to say it I
will say it; if I
have to say it
again
I will say it
again:
remember
Dachau which you said
would never happen
again
even though, in galaxies
of exegesis you have not solved
the there is no contradiction
between mass murder and playing
Schubert thesis.

Since then My Lai,
Kampuchea, paralysis
in the face of ethnic cleansing. If
I have to say it I
will say it. If I
have to say it
again
I will say it
again
for there is no such thing
as compassion fatigue
only compassion
forgetting. If I
have to say it
again

KEVIN CAREY
West Sussex

SIX-YEAR-OLD PARALYSED GIRL IN KOSOVO HOSPITAL, DESERTED BY
HER PARENTS 12 MONTHS AGO. 10 AUGUST 1993.

CHILDREN PLAY BEFORE FRENCH U.N. TROOPS, SARAJEVO, 15 AUGUST 1993

Two Buds

Two buds. One fearful, the other
without fear.
Two Yugoslavias. One cold, the other
warm.
Two Germanies. East and West.
Two Sarajevos. One I walk through and drink in.
The other is in a dream.
Two bells. The bell made of air and the bell
that trembles from loneliness.
Two images. Death and Life. Like two dogs.
One sits, the other growls.
There are two homeless persons. One walks in the woods.
The other spreads a map on a park
bench.
Two oxen. One butts, the other has been killed
in a slaughter-house...
There are two bars. One supplies Washington,
the other minds its own business.
There are two coils of wire. One for a chalet,
and the other for a concentration camp.
Two ammunition boxes. One for balance.
The other against it.
There are two promised lands. Eurovision and Interpol
more genuine than the International.
There are two conversations. One with oneself,
the other with the Galaxy.
There are two cosmic colonies. One produces
matter, the other destroys it.
There are two rhythms. Eros and Africa.
Two deaths. One kills, and the other
jokes.

ADMIRAL MAHIĆ
Sarajevo
Translated by Mario Suško

Stranger

He stands without voice or word
Invited by what has happened between us
Invited by what is unfolding around us
Invited by our fear that we may not remain hidden
Invited by the whispering of our confidential agents

No one wants to drive him away any longer
Day after day he'll settle in our priceless world
Century after century he'll peer through the end of our world
So salty is this ground
So bitter is this nightfall
So harsh is his presence
Without voice or word

He stands
And the sun enters into his crooked shape
My black-sheep brothers

HUSEIN TAHMIŠČIČ
Bosnia / Prague
Translated by Ewald Osers

Goran's Song

(for Goran Stefanovski)

This sonnet doesn't have the first line
Doesn't have a form, a metre, a rhyme,
It's been written in the language broken,
It's the love poem, the sign, the token.

We're disappearing, oh, my dear friend,
That fact we try to avoid
But we cannot avoid the void
This is a living after the end

By warm breath try to break the ice
Which mirrors the faces of our widows
To ease their dark days

The winter is coming
Some houses don't have windows
It's getting cold

Some listen to the humble drumming
And get bold.

HARIS PASOVIĆ
Sarajevo

'Beware the hundred percent loyal'

after César Vallejo 1892-1938

'And what if after so many words
the word itself does not survive!
And what if after so many wings of birds
the motionless bird does not survive!
It would be better, truly
if it were completely eaten away and let us end it!

To have been born to live off our death!
To raise from sky to earth
taken away by disasters
and spy on the moment to extinguish our darkness
                              with our shadow!
Better, frankly,
to be eaten away and nothing more!...

                    ...an unknown land
where for the price of an anaesthetic you pay your life

whatever my alibi explanation
it hurts me because it is so out of place:
this business of walking tightropes...'

ERIC MOTTRAM
London

The poem

he who would not be frustrate of his hope to write well hereafter
in laudable things, ought him selfe to be a true Poem
— MILTON: 'An Apology for Smectymnuus'

Where we were few, the flower audible
our blood not tense or gentle, we were poets.
Us, contemporaries, the ego a pastry-hued ghost.
Its twinkle of ukulele, yet
a grenade's smash. The sun gives the heat
it cannot feel. The poet is on all fours,
misty skin finer
than metre, though syntax in his pact
of understanding
with mercy, supple as a baby's wrist.
From God's sinewy chromosomes,
conscience invisible. We, bitter heat-seeking
animals must make conscience. But touching
whose pain? Slovenly light burns
from a pure heart, I say.

Words about a horse, a cycle's milky
lilac spokes? But jagged conscience, a soul
of broken-up lightning. Majesty
with pride, without conscience? The mirror titters,
the face a tense narcissist.
Now comes darkness, its teeth of noise
the rifle's dental anguish, a man with slugs
of lead dotting
a woman through her waist.

The air pains, yet the sea wanders
the music of this island through the ear.
But the mowed women, the bitter
pregnancies, and their unborn
asphyxiating in the cellarage. My son, my Absoloms,
keep your flesh, and do not go killing. The bronchial foreland
hoists its pines, their fragile arms of lace,
toppling like refugees, the piney cones
in succulent aristocracies of perfume and victimisation.
Their lacey leaves, their ferned breath.
This is Croatia, we are poets, from abroad.

JON SILKIN
Newcastle upon Tyne

The poet, replying to 'just criticism', declines to write 'a poem for Bosnia'

Someone opened his eyes. He saw men
like pollarded trees walking, their poor bodies
one whole wound and bruise.
And there came *a great pang*, from the over-
and-over-ing strokes of that maiming,
the world lopped of its crown,
and the nightingale's tongue bit through.
Ah where, good Jesu? Where were you?
And why did you not come, and dress their wounds?
And he wished to die without words
in a corridor filled with sunlight.

As the bone of the amputee
sang under the saw, in Sarajevo,
she, in her coffin-shaped box
suffered a vision of Christ.
If we could talk to them,
if we could make them see
their enemies as human.
Till he came on his knees,
the towel over his arm,
washing and massaging her feet,
the murderer, Sams.

If by a thousand poems
we could make such small difference.

I saw that jewelled kingfisher again today,
and the dragonflies, selving.
From the war of nature, from famine and death,
endless forms most wonderful are being evolved –
Darwin, with his eye off humanity.
Art too is a creature that kills for food.
It eats the words that should have nourished discourse.
We have enough of it already.
Why bring into the world
one more beautiful, conscience-less animal?

The unjust man unjustices, while poets poet.
Alike, they *go themselves*. Which doesn't help.
Where poetry stops nothing happening,
we should stop writing it.
Find humbler ways to make words work, perhaps.

DONALD ATKINSON
Bedford

In Defence of Making Nothing Happen

How glibly they assume we'll all agree
   on the futility
      of poetry,
our grim confrères who seem to judge the art
   by its utility.
      They'd stop the heart.

They'd seal the lips that voice the daily grief.
   They'd censor common pain.
      They'd ban belief,
compassion, love. They'd throw a Bosnian brick
   at poetry, and claim
      it makes them sick

to read poems while Sarajevo burns.
   But Milton and Wordsworth told
      of their concerns:
grief will have words. The censor with his knife
   is arrogant and cold,
      is anti-life.

MICHAEL HULSE
Cologne

Musée des Beaux Arts Revisited

The first thing I notice is an absence:
Daedalus, clearly seen in black and white
Photographs, his wings stretched out, looking down,
Has no place among the marvellous colours of this original
        indifference;
Sunset, the bluish sea, the bent white legs, the ploughman's full red
        sleeves.
So everyone and everything have turned away,
An allegory of pride which can't include anyone who grieves;
A piety discolouring delight.

I go elsewhere
And find a crucifixion without arms, worm-holed,
So skinny I can count the ribs. Both blood and hair
Have been painted on, but there's a smell of nothing human from
        the gold
Byzantine eyes and lavish torment on display.

Beyond them there's a second Brueghel (Older or Younger, I don't
        know);
A small *Massacre of the Innocents*. In the snow
A baby sprawls in a pool of red.
It's dressed in blue. Dogs sniff each other. A soldier repairs
His boots and a civilian quotes from a law book or scripture
Or a register of births to a captain in full armour
As, close by, a moustachioed fatty draws his sword
His other hand holding up a child who stares

As I stare and stare
Thinking how remote this was, but now how close to home,
Massacres in Bosnia, a place we thought was centuries from here,
The consequence of other tongues, other history unlike our own.
I murmur, '*Majka, sestra, brat i dom,*'

Until I wish for voices to insinuate
Warm weather over the winter landscape
My understanding makes. What if they could?
Snow melts and the rigid fingers of the dead show through what is
        compassionate,
The frosty limits mere seeing gives. All the colours run

In the suave stink of what our charity becomes for us.
The fingers of the dead point everywhere even to the sun
Whose violence burns vainglory and all hope.

Impossible
And beside the point to tell Old Masters what to do.
Yet that first Brueghel, for instance, if only the ship were a fable
Of the delicate informed heart which had somewhere else to go
But instead put about and looked for Icarus.

JAMES SUTHERLAND-SMITH
Prešov, Slovakia

Broadcast

The man winds the reel
like spinning a line,
so everyone can hear the *News*.

He's generating electricity
with names sparking, Izetbegović
or Slobodan; this man-powered dynamo
grinding out the volts.

He's unshaven and will go on
for days, years?…They could switch
the system for a Solid State.

The powerlines are down
from here to Sarajevo;
the truth comes whistling in
at every revolution.

He's winding in the line,
a big fish on the end – Radovan Karadzić
or Ratko Mladić. The man hunched over his radio
stranded on the air.

ROBERT COLE
Westcliff-on-Sea

[Untitled]

'You're listening to the sound of summer
and in the next hour we'll be bringing
you up-to-the-minute reports on brave
little Irma Hadzimuratović as she fights
for her life in a London hospital, as
well as revealing the answer to a
question which baffles us all: why does
scum form on our cups of tea? Now here's
Billy Joel.'

IAN BREAKWELL
London

Posthumous

Whether or not it's true we always
get there just too late
for the real scoop, a shutter
closing on the killer's face,

there's still a desperate sort
of duty getting done in every mug-shot
of the wreckage, burnt-out
street, zoom-lensed victim's house.

DAVID WHEATLEY
Co. Wicklow, Eire

Somewhere

Somewhere, exams over,
a couple lie in long grass,
a coot skulls the shallows.

I am shelling beans,
you are watching tennis,
he is watering flowers in the park.

Summer holds its collective breath
and for an evening
we all might fool ourselves

as smoke rises from gardens,
cats loll in the last
of the sun, but it only needs

that nine o'clock
ON switch for the world's face
to press against our glass

and make grotesque
household fires, cats
left-for-dead on the path

as though this place too
were razed by neighbours...
At bed-time I wander out

into dusk, dew forming,
foxgloves, phlox
premature ghosts. You join me

and we talk of our own
family strife but out there
in the lanes and market towns;

four-in-the-morning streets;
the Underground; the dug-out;
the mountain pass;

something grows huge,
will not quite take shape –
but devours the shadows.

SALLY CARR
Long Crendon, Bucks

83

Bosnia Times: small ad

Wanted: wounded children
to help boost unpopular politician
and poor newspaper sales.
Job offers prompt treatment
in working hospital,
a week's fame, international travel.
Must be polite, photogenic and grateful,
prostrate but fit enough
to recover and return home fast.
(Our Home Office Rules you see.)
Blood on some part of face
and vast seeping bandage desirable.
Agitators need not apply.
This agency is committed
to equal opportunity.

DANIELLE HOPE
London

Answering Machine

I have left my answering machine switched on.
I know there are messages coming in
but I'm plugged into my Walkman,
selecting the next tape
having just flicked off the radio.
A writer's surroundings must be carefully chosen.
News on the hour is the worst kind
of invasion of personal space.
I don't want my atmosphere broken.

There's a click then my voice,
with a veneer of friendliness
as it fends off the world
while pretending to give it a choice.
'If you would like to leave a message
speak clearly after the long tone.'
I'll whizz through later, fast-forwarding
and if I want, I'll get back to them.
After all, this is my home.

Later, the machines become silent.
My last page clatters from the printer
while I think about something to eat.
That new Italian bread from Waitrose,
Brie, coffee, a peach…
After such a good session
I deserve a little treat.
Yards of stuff spew from the fax
half-way down the hall – ridiculous.
Nothing can be as urgent as that.

My answering machine is packed,
ready for milking,
its red light exhaustedly winking.
I will play it back.
There is a huge whispering
like the voices of a thousand children
praying I am at home.
They are at the park, it is late,
there is a man watching.
Too shy to talk to machines
they fade. What I have on my tape
is a dew of flesh, dissolving.

HELEN DUNMORE
Bristol

Pigeons

The morning is swallowed by its headlines:
an old man in Bosnia shot as he scurried
along a path to feed his pigeons.
I try not to see the open mouth
jutting from a black heap of coat.

Going into a room upstairs, I remember
two white pigeons I saw in Ravenna.
How they startled with life,
orange claws gripping the stone rim
of a bowl on a wall in a mausoleum.

For fifteen centuries one has dipped
its beak to drink cool aquamarine;
the other's turned towards a cobalt sky.
What will soothe the cooped pigeons?
In a book I look at the hundreds of tesserae,

follow the shadow lines beneath
wings, the breasts shaped by fingers;
think of two hands blue-rivered
with veins, papered with skin, cupping
the feather softness over beating hearts.

Then I see faces grazed by fear,
slippered feet scrambling up a hill,
a bag of seed split and scattered,
birds' wings frantic behind mesh,
an old man coffined in mud.

MYRA SCHNEIDER
London

Why the '21st child' could not be lifted

The arms
Of newspapers and air-waves were strong
But the twenty-first child was too heavy.

Behind one living eye
The mass grave
Of fourteen thousand dead children.
And behind the other
The mass grave, with its huge spoil heap,
Of every child
Still to be killed in that war.

Maybe all that could have been lifted
With more air-waves
And more sheets of newspaper.
But the twenty-first child also held
In one hand locked with hysteria
Every weapon used by that war.
And in the other
Tibet.

TED HUGHES
Devon

The Alternative War

In the alternative war
the politicians hunt each other in the mountains
with six-shooters, tracked by satellite
for millions of TV screens,
or bang it out at high noon in a Sarajevo street.

The Prime Ministers, Presidents, Chancellors and Generals
stand in the van of their troops,
field any home-made bullets
and scramble across the battlefields
looking for tanks, intercontinental ballistic or surface-to-air missiles,
bazookas, rocket-throwers, megaton bombs
and any old steel bric-à-brac with their labels on.

At the United Nations
top-level discussions of legal niceties are arrested
while officials go off to bind wounds in field ambulances.

There are days of media silence:
no pictures of wounded on the box,
just pictures of Fast Bucks
floating at half mast on the world's flagpoles.

In the alternative wars
international companies go into mourning as they lose money,
and there are no columns of smoking oilwells,
no children are dying of wounds and diarrhoea,
and mass-murderers are not preserved
as buffers against other murderers in the same theatre.

Cormorants feed in clear waters
and squadrons of geese gasp and squawk
in V-formation towards far reaches of fertile shore.

HERBERT LOMAS
Aldeburgh, Suffolk

The Scale of Intensity

1) Not felt. Slight drop in atmospheric pressure. In sensitive individuals, déjà vu, mild amnesia.

2) Detected by persons at rest or favourably placed, i.e. in upper floors, hammocks, cathedrals etc. Leaves rustle.

3) Light sleepers wake. Glasses chink. Hairpins, paperclips display slight magnetic properties. Irritability. Vibration like passing of light trucks.

4) Small bells ring. Small increase in surface tension and viscosity of certain liquids. Vibration like passing of heavy trucks. Civil unrest. Large flags fly.

5) Heavy sleepers wake. Books fall off shelves, doors open. Domestic violence. Furniture overturned. Compasses unreliable. Pendulum clocks stop.

6) Large bells ring. Bookburning. Aurora visible in daylight hours. Unprovoked assaults on strangers. Glassware broken. Loose tiles fly from roof.

7) Weak chimneys broken off at roofline. Waves on small ponds, water turbid with mud. Unprovoked assaults on neighbours. Large static charges built up on windows, mirrors, television screens.

8) Perceptible increase in weight of stationary objects: books, cups, pens heavy to lift. Fall of stucco and some masonry. Systematic rape of women and young girls. Sand craters. Cracks in wet ground.

9) Small trees uprooted. Bathwater drains in reverse vortex. Wholesale slaughter of religious and ethnic minorities. Conspicuous cracks in ground. Damage to reservoirs and underground pipelines.

10) Large trees uprooted. Measurable tide in puddles, teacups, etc. Torture and rape of small children. Irreparable damage to foundations. Rails bend. Sand shifts horizontally on beaches.

11) Standing impossible. Widespread self-mutilation. Corposant visible on pylons, lampposts, metal railings. Most bridges destroyed.

12) Damage total. Large rock masses displaced. Movement of hour hand perceptible.

DON PATERSON
Brighton

Looking the Other Way

'An old man lies dead, shot on his way
to feed his pigeons.' The photo shows his face
the wrong way up, coarsened by newsprint.
Appalled, I stare until he blurs; remember

those two-way faces I used to draw
in my rough book; and the time my lover
lay with his head in my lap, while I traced
each crevice of his upside-down loved face,

till everything at the edge bled out.
And nothing changed, but now I saw
a stranger, the way he looked at me,
unblinking upper lids, bottom lids

blinking upwards. Something reptilian,
sub-human. How could I trust that
blank expanse where mouth and nose
should be, where his hair became beard?

And what I wanted, for a fraction
of an instant, was to wipe him out, this man
innocently getting up to let the cat in;
setting off to feed his pigeons.

FRANCES WILSON
Ware, Herts

Lessons of the War
(after Henry Reed)

Today we have breaking of hearts. Yesterday
We had ethnic cleansing. And tomorrow morning
We shall have what to do after firing the village.
But today we have breaking of hearts. Refugees
Queue at the borders of all of the neighbouring countries,
    And today we have breaking of hearts.

This is the latest agreement, whose purpose
Is beating the clock. Insurgents go rapidly backwards
And forwards assaulting and torching the houses.
They call it re-writing the record. And athletes
Go rapidly backwards and forwards, beating the clock
    In order to re-write the records.

This is your sports field today. And this
Is the long-jump pit whose use you will quickly discover
If we hear anyone singing a national anthem
Or wanting the toilet. Anthems are played by the band
(Who've been to the toilet) for every flag on the flagpole.
    Which in our case we have not got.

SIMON RAE
Devizes

FAMILIES WATCH SICK AND WOUNDED BEING
EVACUATED FROM SARAJEVO, 16 AUGUST 1993

Not the Nine O'clock News
or the National Curriculum

Sarajevo's a burn, or as if, on my own left arm.

It's learning to live without dreams.

'I have a dream…'
I had one. I knew it would keep like a poem.

It's learning to live with the one who cries
at the Nine O'clock News

and feels bereft
and daft

considering. For 44 years she knew she was right about, could prove it,
could even have killed for it

if she'd had a Kalashnikov to hand or any gun
grenade shell bomb with which to express her indignation.

Sarajevo's the stuff
or as if of self-

examination – not the National Curriculum,
the Archduke Ferdinand – the fire this time.

GILLIAN ALLNUTT
Durham

The Minutes of Hasiba
(from an interview on 6 November 1992)

They came at night with their flashlights
Through PARTISANS' HALL
They took me with them and we drove
To a bridge over the Drina
On the bridge stood
Ten older women Tied up
And fifteen soldiers They yelled
Here comes one of yours See how we love her
Then they did everything with me All fifteen of them
Afterwards they smoked and put out their cigarettes
In my hair Then one soldier took
His knife and slit a farmer's throat
Not quite through So that his head stayed on his shoulders
It didn't bother me anymore I had
Seen so much already I didn't care
Then he tore his head off entirely and they played
Soccer with it and laughed and laughed
I knew the farmers They were
Neighbours colleagues relatives
Just a few weeks ago I knew most
Of the soldiers too They were
Neighbours colleagues relatives They were
Men like you

HOLGER TESCHKE
Berlin
Translated from the German by Margitt Lehbert

Poor Tom at Vukovar

I saw poor Tom completely mad
on peak-time TV live last night
from Vukovar. Straight from Baghdad
the BBC's reporter questioned him

inside a church that was shelled-out;
asked for his personal response to rout.
Even a dubbed translation could not close
the obvious distress war had exposed.

His mind refused to recognise landscapes
shelling had sluiced to new contours.
He talked wildly of rape,
torture and grief, aerial spores

that settled on the city through the day.
All his metaphors jumbled and crazy,
the cameraman panned sideways and away
to a shot of smoke drifting hazily.

STEPHEN SMITH
Croydon

Vukovar

October 14th 1991: for the third day humanitarian aid
was prevented from reaching people in ruined Vukovar.

I had an apparition of Vukovar and I took a walk for a few streets –
around the block – with my hands frozen – up to the tobacco shop
and on returning I thought so that's the way they used

to sail back again into the damp – illuminated coldly
and precisely by the European streetlights –
those travellers around the world who were believed

dead straight – about food recipes – about people's mysteries
– about doors to treasures and about absolutely all the numbers –
yet everyone remained misunderstood and broken to the end

because of the story about the wolfish eyes
dazzled by white glare – a guard
of life and death – perhaps the very live death already –

and so you yourself came home – and for this relentless gift
relentless to the last breath – unaccented in languages of Europe
from the stones of Ireland to the Caucasian stones – it's in vain

repeating to the European tobacconists the civilities of merchant
adventurers – how the storm's approaching – which is the storm
of silence – and how with meteorological accuracy piles of news

from day to day will be picked up out of hands
together with ashes and rain mud and snow by the wolfish silence
from everywhere to everywhere Vukovar Vukovar Vukovar Vukovar

VENO TAUFER
Slovenia
Translated by the author with Jo Shapcott

Crossings

The woman running, bends low, crossing
from one street corner to another.
She wears a blue dress speckled
with small white flowers,
a white cardigan that flaps
around her back when she runs.
Under her arm she squeezes a sports bag
with pink stripes containing freshly
washed nappies for her neighbour's child.
Her name is Nevza.
An old, fat man sets off
for the corner she has just left.
He is slow and cannot bend,
he rolls from side to side
troubled by his old war wound.
His grandchildren call him Papa.
He falls and does not move.
A young girl, Nilena, follows him.
She is fast and crosses in a flash,
jumps for the pavement, fist
punching the air with rage.
Nevza, Papa, Nilena.
The innocence of names and language,
vowels and consonants shaped by the mouth.
Sarajevo, Garazde, Omarska.
The threshold of meanings formed
by the mind, evocative sounds,
language stooped low, bent double,
crossing into death.

JOHN MURPHY
London

Difficult Times

These are difficult times. April arrived
through a rush of rain. In the train window
a newspaper – fingers at either side –
skimmed, superimposed, across a landscape
bereft of houses. A child's charred hand dropped
out of focus – emerged from a long
pool of waste water, and was folded up,
left on the seat.

We are watching this war
on a far away screen without the sound.
Nothing seems to matter more than the rain.
As we left that train the city filled with
workers and shoppers, doing whatever
passes for life.

The value of pity
sinks slowly in our purses and pockets;
we edge along pavements. In a minute,
someone anywhere might be blown to pieces:
it's all either cowardice or courage.
Daily, new mothers are wielding pushchairs,
thrusting their offspring out, ahead of them,
into the face of oncoming traffic.

MARION LOMAX
Berkshire

The Moon Rises at Midnight

Moonrise at midnight
searches earth like a cave,
A crime has occurred,
there's a knife on the doorsill.

A red moonrise
searches all the wells.
A crime has occurred
there's blood in the well.

The moon wanes to dark.
Nothing has occurred.
Night, merely, and a tarn's eye
and wolf-light and a footfall

and on the doorsill a fish,
and a slashed oak,
stone of the blood and a covered well,
and hypnosis of iron.

EEVA-LIISA MANNER
Tampere, Finland
Translated from the Finnish by Herbert Lomas

Sarajevo Night

Everything has run out: words, water, sleep.
In the darkness he tries to read the heavens
but smoke rubs out the familiar
sieve of light. It's a sky like broken slate,
where language has disintegrated
and fallen chalky to the sea,
to the tide's easy chatter,
to the moon's pull on its mirror,
and it's my sky too.

His mouth is dry and mine is silent.
Spit it out, shape the difficult syllables,
he needs a new voice
new words in a new language.
Without that how can he use the forbidden water,
slake his thirst, soak a rag
and wipe clean his cracked window
that we may all look out and see where to begin?

MAURA DOOLEY
London

Someone in Sarajevo

Someone in Sarajevo is dreaming
of his grandmother asleep in the armchair
they chopped for wood for last winter.
A woman dreams the city is under a lake
and she must swim to the bakery each morning.
A fifteen-year-old boy is dreaming
that he's just walked naked into a classroom
and all his friends are laughing at him.
A professor dreams he has eaten all his books
and no one asked him why.
An old woman dreams of fields of wheat
locked in a burning house.
And a young woman dreams of her brother
back from the smokey hills, his green uniform
wet from collar to ankle. So wet
the green is almost black.

MICHAEL BLACKBURN
Lincoln

Skeins o geese

Skeins o geese write a word
across the sky. A word
struck like a gong
afore I wis born.
The sky moves like cattle, lowin.

I'm as empty as stane, as fields
ploo'd but not sown, naked
an blin as a stane. Blin
tae the word, blin
tae a' soon but geese ca'ing.

Wire twists lik archaic script
roon a gate. The barbs
sign tae the wind as though
it was deef. The word whustles
ower high for ma senses. Awa

no lik the past which lies
strewn aroun. Nor sudden death.
No' like a lover we'll ken
an connect wi forever.
The hem of its goin drags across the sky.

Whit dae birds write on the dusk?
A word niver spoken or read.
The skeins turn hame,
on the wind's dumb moan, a soun,
maybe human, bereft.

KATHLEEN JAMIE
Newburgh, Fife

Leaf Soup

You must tell me the names of your trees.
No, I'm a cook. I had a restaurant.
No, only the cellar. Twenty-three days
we hid, my mother, sister, children. I can't
eat so much, thank you. Spring? It was cold.
We lived in the woods all May. Slept in the car.
My husband? A chef in the Army. He told
us to go. Sometimes I wonder how far
we are from Sarajevo. It's okay.
I'm glad my children have beds, proper floors;
we tore ours up to keep warm. It's good they play,
race their new toys up and down the corridors.
Already I think my son is getting fatter.
I did my best, but it was always bitter.

People keep coming with cameras.
I don't like the flashes. They took us,
Nejra, Martina and me, squashed up
on a washing machine from a chap
called Norweb who seemed to be two men.
It's better here. We can shout and run.
People come to the front door with food
and clothing. Mother says she'll go mad
if they ask her any more questions.
All yesterday she kept the curtains
shut, stayed in our room. I took some soup
but she wouldn't eat it, fell asleep
so Nejra and me played out the back
digging, scooping leaves into our truck.

PATRICIA POGSON
Kendal

Supper
(a childhood picture)

Bread and herbs on the table,
pieces of bread,
lumps of earth,
hunks of my father's hands,
the shadow of Zekonja's tongue
hung out.

And a jar of water.
And a star which has made an error
in space.
And a star falling through
the window and vanishing
in the jar's clay.

And my father, my mother, myself
illuminated by that very
star.

DRAGOLJUB JEKNIĆ
Bosnia
Translated by Mario Suško

Child's Play

Last night I heard the men out back clicking their tongues
tut-tutting over fighting in some foreign land.
It could never happen here. They nodded,
sitting side by side, sipping chilled brandy.
How could 40 years of friendship, turn to hate?

Cold stars in a silent night. Brother, they called themselves.
Their voices one song you're not allowed to sing, being outside
the circle of men. One of them is your brother,
the old one your father's father, dark eyes, mud
in the bottom of the cup. The Turkish taste sugar-lump sweet.

Earlier in the day, chasing my little brother into the forest
I hate you I hate you I hate you, I wish you were dead.
All for the sake of a wooden doll, such reds, such blues.
I saw red, ran after him, might have killed him.
Can words kill? The priest says they can. Cross my heart hope to die.

Yesterday I was a little girl, wondering *will I be pretty?*
will the boys notice me? Today I chop off my hair,
disguise myself as my dead brother. I take on his swagger,
wear his mean look, hope the men don't see me
pick up his weapon. Little brother, such a big gun.

Step on a crack you break your mother's back.
How many must I have stepped on. There is no one left to forgive me.
My heart is a concrete bunker, nothing can get in.
My enemy wears a familiar face, calls me by my name,
pats me on the head, promises the impossible. I shoot what moves.

Cow wandered off. She crossed six borders on the way to the stream,
six more when she stepped in. Hiccup and you're on the wrong side.
They've got the salt, we've got the pepper. We've got the pastry
they've got the filling. I'm used to the guns now, it's just the killing.
Just the silence that frightens me. I play hopscotch with the dead.

One potato two potato three potato four.
Mother used to say I talked too much. Now I don't talk at all.
Five potato six potato seven potato more. Wish I could take all
          this hate
turn it into water, take a long drink of forgetfulness. There's no end.
Stack hands, tit for tat, tag – you're it – the games we play.

JUDI BENSON
London

Lament

To give birth meant nothing to us.
My younger brothers, I do not remember all their names.

You were like earth
Perhaps that's why your lap was so warm.

Every autumn your white peasant skirt
Reddened from giving birth.

What colour was your hair?
The black kerchief reminded me of bread.

You decanted all springs on your back
If I knew where you lie buried I'd drive the earth to tears.

DARA SEKULIĆ
Bosnia
Translated by Mario Suško

No Man's Land

Where is the country she's exploring: it has no borders.
Its name is edge. Neighbours march down her streets,
their soldiers' boots beating poisonous tattoos
in pursuit of cleansing, antiseptic illusion of enema.

Every exit is blocked with bodies, passport control.
The sky in her ears is streaked with the whine of jets,
blind to the planet's sacred anatomy of blood and bone.

She wanted to record history according to the facts,
thought the present was a safe stop en route to the future.
Until she saw the stains on her fingers from the ashes
of all the books they burnt. Then terror was the colour
of blood behind her eyes when the general punched her
after she'd screwed up the courage to tell him
how scared she was. She caught the crimson in her hands,
saw it drain away into the carpet, absorbing atrocities
like a camcorder on R & R. She's stuck in a gully
called Bliss/Paralysis. Her shoes are full of stones.

Out there is where the air is sour as the breath
of how many soldiers on orders to rape her, her
and her children. They have no map of their future.

One day at a time in an emergency. And the ambulances
with their engines doctored wail like women
in a classical tragedy, strident blue sirens, all eyes
and ears, open as wounds. There's something wrong
no one can put right, despite the U.N. Forces,
the designer diplomats. She's tried all the options.

But there's no new thing under the sun, its orange ball
of flame roaring its warning like a boy scout collecting
shillings in return for a badge his mother will stitch
on his sleeve before his arm is blown off in an incident
in the marketplace. His mother will be the last to be told.

She wished she'd stayed at home and watched it on television.
Sometimes she even thought she was. And was blood
really that red, the colour they used to mark borders.

LINDA FRANCE
Hexham, Northumberland

Toys for the War Child

The first toy is silence, in a freezing camp, on a mountain of rags,
beneath shredded trees waiting for aid lorries
or soldiers who steal even the silence.

The second toy is words, a code bony as a knuckle of hatred, screaming
commands of destruction, derision, deceit, small flags of meaning
to hang between surges of hunger.

The third toy is a song that you must bite on when they beat you,
memorise when you eat insects or grass, a bunch of blades in your
            belly,
the song stinging the stitches in your soul.

The fourth toy is a branch that you will learn to shape into a cudgel,
            a spear,
a man trap, a javelin of flame; you will run with it, lunge,
play dirty tricks, twist it through human flesh.

And then you will take the silence, the words, the song and the
            ancient weapon
leaping from nakedness into an armour of revenge, plastering
            medals all
over your pride, stamping your feet in your brother's eyes.

DAVID GRUBB
Henley on Thames

The Wedding

He has no right arm or left leg
to bring to his wedding

but friends and relatives are here
and each has brought a present

and he can twist to kiss his wife
before they cut the cake

baked with eggs that someone found,
each one a month's salary.

MATTHEW SWEENEY
London

Enemies

I do not know who my enemies are.
Is he Shrap Nel. He is sharp
and he bites me. It was he
who opened the door to Menin
Gococci. You can see him
under a microscope, if you care to look.
They say I am fighting him,
but I don't know who I am fighting.
Am I, then, an animal in a circus?
I can levitate, with others like me
and fly to In Tensive Care.
How do you say that?
My mother has gone away,
my father strokes my aching head
as I rush in and out of the dark.
I am called Irma, one of the chosen,
and I have an Oper Ation
named after me. Oper Ations
are what I know about, as they free me
from Shrap Nel and send in Anti Biotics
to fight the bad Menin Gococci.
If I live I shall still be Muslim.
If I die, war will be my enemy,
culler of the cutest, PR job.
Is he an enemy too?
So many.

ELIZABETH BARTLETT
Burgess Hill, West Sussex

Striking Distance

Was there one moment when the woman
who's always lived next door turned stranger
to you? In a time of fearful weather,
did the way she laughed, or shook out her mats
make you suddenly feel as though
she'd been nursing a dark side to her difference,
and bring that word, in a bitter rush
to the back of the throat – *Croat/Muslim/
Serb* – the name, barbed, ripping
its neat solution through common ground?

Or has she acquired an alien patina
day by uneasy day, unnoticed
as fall-out from a remote explosion?
So you don't know quite when you came to think
the way she sits, or ties her scarf,
is just like a Muslim/Serb/Croat;
and she uses their word for water-melon
as usual, but now it's an irritant
you mimic to ugliness in your head,
surprising yourself in a savage pleasure.

Do you sometimes think, she could be you,
the woman who's trying to be invisible?
Do you have to betray those old complicities
– money worries, sick children, men?
Would an open door be too much pain
if the larger bravery is beyond you
(you can't afford the kind of recklessness
that would take, any more than she could);
while your husband is saying you don't understand
those people/Serbs/Muslims/Croats?

One morning, will you ignore her greeting
and think you see a strange twist to her smile
– for how could she not, then, be strange to herself
(this woman who lives nine inches away)
in the inner place where she'd felt she belonged,
which, now, she'll return to obsessively
as a tongue tries to limit a secret sore?

And as they drive her away, will her face
be unfamiliar, her voice, bearable:
a woman crying from a long way off?

CAROLE SATYAMURTI
London

Airlift

I'm playing aeroplanes,
Airlifting my child into
A sky so clear so blandly blue

Palm pressed to palm,
My feet against his chest
Lifting; he is a parachutist

Reversed, freefaller
Rising, limbs spreadeagled
In the void that's prodigal

Of headroom as the halls
Of death. Steady and hard
Against my soles his eightmonth heart

Beats, the ribcage supple
As any bird's, less frail
More vulnerable. Hearts fail

When death's a way of life.
Words fail. I close my grip
For the descent, the earth in eclipse.

ELIZABETH GARRETT
Oxford

From Caspar Hauser

We never sleep. We have no empty squares.
It would be impossible to deliver him
So he stood out. The wars

Blow children up. Some fall our way.
They know a single sentence. They can say
My father is dead in somewhere in the news,

My mother raped and dead, or thrust it down
In somebody else's capitals
Over our headlines in the underground,

Or howl, just that: a particular girl
Rides the loop, stop by stop,
And holds a stump out and a begging cup

And howls, just that. I have observed her eyes.
They are so absent you would say she hires
Herself as a professional keener in her cause.

And nobody looks at anyone else, we all
Pray there'll be no hold-up for the howl
Cannot be borne beyond its usual

Measure. And much the same
Like wreckage after a catastrophe we have not fathomed yet
Children of our own making squat

Along the concrete walkways and the bridges
We cross to the opera
And hold a cardboard in their laps that says

What their state is.

DAVID CONSTANTINE
Oxford

112

The Mothers

Imagine a town, a southern town
in high summer. Imagine the sweet break
of strawberry on the tongue, at a table,
in a café, at the innermost cleft
of one of those street corners near the sea.

And then imagine the woman,
her daughter poised like a bird across
the table, candles adrift in her eyes,
a starlit birth she can't remember.
It stretches dark and tasting faintly of fruit
beyond the rim of the table, the door's jamb,
the smallholding of their twenty years together.

You cannot imagine, as this frosted birthday-cake
splits on each tongue and juices stain their
twisting lips, how wide the mouth that utters
forth its howl, how another woman's fingers
claw at all that rubble, just one shoe,
a single leg like stone, the less-than-grown
sweet belly of her black and charcoaled daughter.

The morning after, the English mother, licked through
with strawberries and the night's long limb of sex,
lifts a golliwog from the box outside the bric-à-brac shop.
She thinks of marmalade, peeling the golliwogs
among her grandmother's blue and marbled shadows,
picks up the doll and stares at his grinning face.
Just as the ground in Sarajevo gapes again
to swallow black blood and brackish water,
just as the Bosnian mother holds the taste of birth
upon her tongue, just once before her face cracks,
the horizon splits and the belovèd world is cloven.

As though the fault-line runs in memory beyond
all sense, tearing through Bosnia to the seaside town
where the knife eases through sugar, a woman wishing
with the weight of all her futures, still intact.

NICKI JACKOWSKA
Brighton

113

Child Burial

Your coffin looked unreal,
fancy as a wedding cake.

I chose your grave clothes with care,
your favourite stripey shirt,

your blue cotton trousers.
They smelt of woodsmoke, of October,

your own smell there too.
I chose a gansy of handspun wool,

warm and fleecy for you. It is
so cold down in the dark.

No light can reach you and teach you
the paths of wild birds,

the names of the flowers,
the fishes, the creatures.

Ignorant you must remain
of the sun and its work,

my lamb, my calf, my eaglet,
my cub, my kid, my nestling,

my suckling, my colt, I would spin
time back, take you again

within my womb, your amniotic lair,
and further spin you back

through nine waxing months
to the split seeding moment

you chose to be made flesh,
word within me.

I'd cancel the love feast
the hot night of your making.

I would travel alone
to a quiet mossy place,

you would spill from me into the earth
drop by bright red drop.

PAULA MEEHAN
Dublin

Flower Aid

Here it is summer.
Our gardens are full of flowers
but even if we air-lifted

every bloom
from every garden in Cornwall
there wouldn't be enough flowers

to cover their graves;
and even if we wove all our flowers
into one fragrant rope

it wouldn't be strong enough
to rescue a single orphan.

Here thousands of us weep
in our kitchens at every newscast,
but in Bosnia thousands don't weep,

they just go on mining the orchards.
Over there, snipers rake the gardens.

There will never be enough flowers.
The orchards explode, in memory of...

PENELOPE SHUTTLE
Falmouth

Danilo Blagojević

Monday

Danilo come from Sarajevo:
only eleven, he sits in my class
and clumsies open his English book
                at Page 2.

He is clean-nosed, clever, but – for once –
is not concentrating on my foreign voice.
This morning, he continues to look
out of an unbroken window.

Tuesday

His parents do not come from Sarajevo:
being besieged, they do not know
how seriously he sits in my class
and tries to compose story
about small dog
who love to bark at birds...
Maybe, his teacher should stress
that he must be using the article
and writing in the present tense
                by Key Stage 2.

Danilo, though of few words,
is also under siege:
at lunch-time, his class-mates insist
on including him in their league.
He rolls up his second-hand sleeve
and fingertips a familiar pawn
towards his foreign adversary
in friendly international.
He cannot wait for the return...

Wednesday

Danilo do not go to assembly:
after all, he is an atheist
who has no faith in the silence

and does not believe
in the snowless window,
its unshattered hopes...

                        In his trance,
he continues to look
across the January slopes
where his class-mates still ski
in cyrillic calligraphy;
in the dead silence, he see
dog barking at birds.

PETER CASH
Stoke-on-Trent

White-out

Blindingly from the east, blizzards come.
The first flakes sizzle on the stove,
as the storm gathers momentum.
Were we in such a land, my love...

It is of you we think, children of Bosnia,
your ghosts like white birds passing
over, passing over: so that already
the sky is black with your wings.

STEWART CONN
Edinburgh

The Field-Mouse

Summer, and the long grass is a snare drum.
The air hums with jets.
Down at the end of the meadow,
far from the radio's terrible news,
we cut the hay. All afternoon
its wave breaks before the tractor blade.
Over the hedge our neighbour travels his field
in a cloud of lime, drifting our land
with a chance gift of sweetness.

The child comes running through the killed flowers,
his hands a nest of quivering mouse,
its black eyes two sparks burning.
We know it will die and ought to finish it off.
It curls in agony big as itself
and the star goes out in its eye.
Summer in Europe, the fields hurt,
and the children kneel in long grass,
staring at what we have crushed.

Before day's done the field lies bleeding,
the dusk garden inhabited by the saved, voles,
frogs, a nest of mice. The wrong that woke
from a rumour of pain won't heal,
and we can't face the newspapers.
All night I dream the children dance in grass
their bones brittle as mouse-ribs, the air
stammering with gunfire, my neighbour turned
stranger, wounding my land with stones.

GILLIAN CLARKE
Llandyssul, Dyfed

Yellow Plates

The family moving into the house were told
    to make themselves at home.

But dropping their things in a heap in the bare centre
    of the largest, warmest room,

they had wondered how in hell they could cook a meal
    for twelve in a strange kitchen

(what with the brothers so drunk on the national drink
    and the grandchildren

wailing the infant anthems 'Why is Nobody
    Looking at Me Alone'

or 'Take the Others Away Until I Need Them'
    or 'What's Undone's Undone')

but they found the cooking terribly easy, for here
    was a fridge, a working oven

with even a clock, and here was a pile of matching
    yellow plates: five, six, seven.

GLYN MAXWELL
Welwyn Garden City

The Cupboard

Her grandmother's cupboard is made
of painted cedar. She remembers
– how old was she five? – unpegging
stiff boards of white sheets,
bleached from the sun, folding them
into the wicker basket in the yard.
And the singed steaming of cotton
cooling on the backs of chairs.
Then up the dark stairs to pile
them neat as stone slabs. One shelf
always kept for winter blankets
smelling of camphor.

She loved the doves in each corner
of the doors, a floral garland
strung from beak to beak, the swirls
of eucalyptus leaves.
A garden to get lost in.

Now winter is coming.
Last night the wind blew her candle out
broken glass rattles in the panes
like ill fitting teeth. There has been
nothing to eat for weeks. The neighbours
rumour of snipers, of convoys, they say
Hassan's lorry couldn't get through.

In the corner she watches her daughter
Jasna huddled in her brother's big coat,
poking out the bullet eyes of old potatoes
– her own mother lies under a fresh
mound of earth. And in the dim lamp-light,
as she scrapes the green skins, she knows
that there will be no more laughter
of mothers, of daughters unpegging
sun-dried sheets in the yard.

The cold is burning their fingers,
the cold is turning their chapped
hands red. Yet still she would give

her daughter a garden to walk in
a garden of eucalyptus and doves...

From the back of the chair she quietly
takes her scarf and wraps it
around her shoulders. From the hook
in the yard she fetches the axe.

SUE HUBBARD
London

Exile

The old land swinging in her stomach
she must get to know this language
better – key words, sound patterns
wordgroups of fire and blood.

Try your classmates with
the English version of your name.
Maria. Try it.
Good afternoon. How are you?

I am fine. Your country –
you see it in a drop of water.
The last lesson they taught you there
was how to use a gun.

And now in stops and starts
you grow a second city in your head.
It is Christmas in this school.
Sarajevo is falling through

a forest of lit-up trees,
cards and decorations.
Mountains split with gunfire
swallow clouds, birds, sky.

MONIZA ALVI
London

Jasmina's House

We count the seconds after the thunder
till smoke puffs up and blackbirds scatter
down the valley. From there the track rises
to our crossroads, where the way divides:

north to the white town, next the top road
haunted by irregulars from either side, then
the other snaking to the pass through rock
St Sava milked to feed his wolf militiamen,

its limestone crumbling to dust with the bones
and tattered clothes of fleeing villagers.
Armoured dragons terrify the crossroads;
grinding up the hill, they swivel sharply,

stare right through our doorless broken house,
our windows emptier than eye sockets,
to where those blackbirds rise like gunsmoke
or damnation over the outer suburbs of hell.

This room was Adnan's, whose skull wobbles
below like a bleached and bearded turnip
in the gully rubble, a flutter of peonies
pleading around him, red as bullet-holes.

I remember how our butcher Ensud
wagged a finger to drive home a point,
snatching it back to tip his scales.
We paid dearly for our meat.

Ensud knifed my brother too, and cousin Budo,
but left my mother for the Milanović brothers
who used to sell her milk. They tipped
her body down the well, then came for me.

My ransacked room is silent but for mice
tearing at my hairbrush for their nests
(they'll need my hair when winter comes).
As blood hardens on the wooden floor

my body's shape is leaving the bed,
rain easing it back into a mattress slab.
A cold wind rustles through my school papers,
the diary splayed open where it fell,

pages blurring into blackness as the ink
spreads, marking my life at the front,
leaving blank the lost white months
of empty time, from June to December.

REBECCA HAYES
Paris

The Desire Paths of Sarajevo

People ask, 'Why do you work on film and theatre? Isn't this
crazy?' I always answer, 'There is a reason to make art.
Only love can lighten things. What we do is produce love.'
I haven't had a shower in eight months.

— HARIS POSOVIĆ, festival producer, Sarajevo

He'd had a research project: the Indo-China *rage*.
He knew the folk-cure. A raw ruby, the bigger
the better, slung round the throat in salt.
As near the heart as possible.

But for all his mother's lore
that started him off on this kick
– the little-petalled rue
picked at night from white ledges

on Mount Belasnija – he knew his stuff.
He'd been to medical school. Zagreb, Karachi,
London. He'd been on the trail
of phibellasomes in the immune system,

suspended between two leaves of Boston glass:
his bench-space in the lab at Sarajevo.
He'd had a woman too. Whom he might have been
going to marry. But they'd worried sex would fade

if they'd had kids. And she'd wanted work.
She'd trained in RADA. They met in Burlington Arcade,
both window-shopping, bored, both dreaming of
impossibly sweet *raki*, the pear *raki* you only get

from trees on Mount Igman, served warm with *burek*
in Bas-Carsija. Later, home, they'd joked
on small salaries about a basement in Dobjinje.
A house open to all. She had a scar now,

a strawberry sabre up her inner thigh,
where the shell that ground her mother
and sisters into their flat, had left
its saltlick. He'd sewn it – an Oxfam needle –

but rarely saw it. Only in half hours
off the amputating table. These August nights,
while the rest of Europe's lovers, he supposed,
where spotting Leonids

from windows that still had glass, he'd lie out
with her on rough ground between burnt cars.
Mortars give cover. He slept in corridors:
couldn't take her there. And she'd moved in

with her idiot aunt. Noise? They hardly noticed.
He'd keep his hand still, to tease.
Three fingers in her. Sniper fire
Morse-coding the flashpoint summer stars.

* * *

He's followed Mujo's tunnel rats
(who've brought him so many stretchers
from the hills) out to today's front line.
Ninety miles from her. Mostar. Three days

of mountain skyline, dodging Browning 5.7s
to the hospital they said they'd help in shifts.
With the last diesel, the Kadzistani generator
pumps flow from the Neretva, rilling

gastro-colitis through a Braille of homes.
Nine-year-old Upha, face purple in the basement
candlelight. Her shrapnel cuts seep rubies
from their bindings, to her leg.

What he hangs onto is one night – they'd still
had electricity, he'd still had a room –
when the Vice-President howled on radio
like a moonstruck wolf. The night Sekaković

told General Kikanjac Go fuck himself
or he'd blow the hydro-electric plant
sky-high over Visegrad. The night they knew
things had got mad. No backturn. And he'd knelt up

above her, parting her, two hands in a soft
karate chop, staring in at her pink shadows,
before his kiss, his tongue, her salt
became the only things. Sea-level. A burning.

* * *

I thought I saw this, standing with my safe child
on my old lover's balcony. Swollen suburbs.
A near-full moon beyond this city's wall
over Mount Iouktas: its radar profile

of a safely buried god. Marilen and Niko
argue in whispers over nappies unavailable
in Sarajevo. If this was Mostar? Maybe
I've got it wrong. None of us are...

...and who's inventing who? Imagining,
all the same. If this was us? Your fingers,
in me out there on rough ground, under shadows
of uprooted oleanders, *lyra*-backed bouzouki.

If it was us drinking, you teasing
in Novi Pazar, under the pierced
milk-alabaster of the old bazaar,
where pigs and geese once fought for space,

where woodcarvings and leatherware
glowed in the black-finned lamps,
where now old newspapers, *Oslobodenje*,
Le Monde, The Herald Tribune, Al-Ahram,

Frankfurter Allgemeine Zeitung,
telling like Roman astronomers
so many coffee-cup hopes,
are skittering in hot wind?

RUTH PADEL
Heraklion, August 1993

Desire paths: town-planning term. The paths people make for
themselves through a city. Not pre-patterned by an architect.

All things are connected.

You must teach your children that the ground
beneath their feet is the ashes of our grandfathers.
So that they will respect the land, tell your children
that the earth is rich with the lives of our kin.
Teach your children what we have taught our children,
that the earth is our mother.
Whatever befalls the earth befalls the sons of the earth.
If men spit upon the ground, they spit upon themselves.

This we know. The earth does not belong to man;
man belongs to the earth. This we know.
All things are connected like the blood which unites one family.
All things are connected.

Whatever befalls the earth befalls the sons of the earth.
Man did not weave the web of life; he is merely a strand in it.
Whatever he does to the web, he does to himself.

– from the speech of Chief Seattl of the Suquamish to the President
of the United States, 1854, on the proposal that they surrender
their ancestral lands to the whites and leave for a reservation.

ACKNOWLEDGEMENTS

The editors wish to thank *The Independent* for generous assistance in the preparation and production of this book. The following poems appeared in *The Independent*'s *Bosnia Poems* series: Susan Bassnett's untitled poem, Michael Blackburn's 'Someone in Sarajevo', Joseph Brodsky's 'Bosnia Tune', Alan Brownjohn's 'In Moslodina', Derek Power's 'Flying the Flag in Bosnia', Simon Richey's 'The Encounter', Haris Pasovic's 'Goran's Song', and Ken Smith's 'Essential Serbo-Croat'.

Further acknowledgements are due to: Anvil Press Poetry Ltd for permission to reprint Tadeusz Różewicz's 'Posthumous Rehabilitation' from *They came to see a poet* (1992), and for Marius Kociejowski's 'Night Patrol' from *Doctor Honoris Causa* (1993); to Bloodaxe Books Ltd for Ken Smith's 'Essential Serbo-Croat' from *Tender to the Queen of Spain* (1993) and Stephen Smith's 'Poor Tom at Vukovar' from *The Fabulous Relatives* (1993); to the Gallery Press for Paula Meehan's 'Child Burial' from *The Man who was Marked by Winter* (1991); to the Menard Press for the foreword quotation from Ivo Andric; to *Sarajevo Witness* for Adrian Mitchell's 'Peace Memories of Sarajevo'; to Seren Books for Tony Curtis's 'From the hills, the town' from *Taken for Pearls* (1993).

And to the following publications in which several of these poems first appeared: to *Guardian Weekend* for Simon Rae's 'Lessons of the War'; to *The Irish Review* for Ian Duhig's 'A Basket of Dalmatian Oysters'; to *London Magazine* for Tony Flynn's 'The Sentence'; to *New Republic* for Czeslaw Milosz's 'Sarajevo'; to *The Observer* for Myra Schneider's 'Pigeons'; to *Poetry Review* for Carole Satyamurti's 'Striking Distance' and Jo Shapcott's 'War and Peace'; to *Slow Dancer* for Heather Spears' 'The Search for Scarlett'; to *Tandem* for Linda France's 'No Man's Land'; to *The Times Literary Supplement* for Kathleen Jamie's 'Skeins o geese'.

The editors' special thanks are due to Mario Susko, formerly of Sarajevo, now at the University of East Anglia, for his help and advice. Of the Bosnian poets in this anthology the poems by Admiral Mahic, Dragoljub Jeknic, Dara Sekulic and Abdulah Sidran appeared in *Contemporary Poetry of Bosnia and Herzegovina*, edited and translated by Mario Susko (International Peace Centre and the P.E.N. Centre, Sarajevo, 1993); poems by Ahmed Muhamed Imamovic, Josip Osti, Mario Susko and Marko Vesovic appeared in *Books from Bosnia and Herzegovina* (Ljubljana, Slovenia, no date available), translated by Mario Susko. Miljenko Jergovic's 'Concentration Camp' appeared first in his collection *Himmel Commando*; Husein Tahmscic's 'Stranger' first appeared in *Prospice*. 'Bosnia Tune' by Joseph Brodsky © Joseph Brodsky, first appeared in *The New York Times*, 18 November 1992; reprinted by permission of Farrar, Straus & Giroux Inc.